Essential Chinese

Learning Chinese with Fun

基础汉语
中文益智宫

Joy Betz and Chong An Chang

Kendall Hunt
publishing company

Cover image © Shutterstock Inc.

www.kendallhunt.com
Send all inquiries to:
4050 Westmark Drive
Dubuque, IA 52004-1840

Copyright © 2013 by Joy Betz and Chong An Chang

ISBN 978-1-4652-1519-2

Printed in the United States of America
10 9 8 7 6 5 4 3 2 1

Table of Contents

Preface

This book, ***Essential Chinese --- Learning Chinese with Fun***, is the first book in a series written for North American learners who wish to study the Chinese language and literature. The book contains 14 lessons with short stories and fun exercises to help learners readily grasp the meaning of the language as well as appreciate the nuances in its applications. These unique features set this book apart from other textbooks currently on the market.

Although various Chinese textbooks are available, most of them are designed for beginners. Entry level textbooks usually pay attention to the practical aspects such as how to communicate in an airport, at a bus stop, in a store, or in a restaurant. These books are useful and practical, but readers may not be able to move beyond the technical aspects to enjoy the beauty of the language and develop an understanding for the literature.

Our books are themselves good articles worth reading. We focus on generating reader interest and linking language skills with advanced grammar, and literary application such as idioms. Learners can progress at a steady and continuous pace by following the lessons contained in this and the coming books in our series: *Essential Chinese --- Learning Chinese with Fun; Intermediate Chinese --- Learning Chinese with Science;* and *Advanced Chinese --- Understanding China.*

In this book, each lesson has a list of words, questions, and exercises. Every lesson contains two parts: the *Main Text* and the *Practical Chinese*. The practical part is designed to help the students handle situations such as "greetings", "shopping", "at a party", and get used to oral communications. If the learner still needs basic training in speaking Chinese, he/she can bypass the

Main Text and concentrate on the *Practical Chinese* first. If basic Chinese (greetings, etc.) is already mastered, concentrating on the *Main Text* will help them enjoy the rich contents of this book fully. This offers flexibility for learners at all levels and enables the teaching professional to take a more personalized, learner-based approach.

Some texts of this book were based on well-known jokes or ancient fable stories. To them we added English explanation, Chinese *pinyin*, table of words, table of idioms, questions, illustrations, and discussion. Other texts were fully created and written by us. The authors have both received formal training in the Chinese language and have extensive experience in teaching courses in USA and Canada. These books are suitable for Chinese courses at various levels offered in North America. We welcome input and feedback from readers in order to make continued improvements.

Joy Betz (USA)
Chong An Chang (Canada)

序

　　这本中文教材**基础汉语 --- 中文益智宫**，是给在北美的汉语学习者编写的，一共 14 课，风格生动有趣，由许多笑话和幽默小故事组成，启发智慧让人更为聪明。全书课文逐步加深自成体系，内涵丰富，教师可以选择使用。

　　虽然现在有各种汉语教材问世，但是多数都是入门程度，注重实用，教读者在不同的场合（见面、机场、银行、商店、旅行、餐馆、家庭等等）该怎么说话的基本教材，内容多是"你好"、"请问"、"我是..."等等的基本口语训练。这些课本相当实用，但是文学性不强。读者还不能从中欣赏中文的美好。

　　这本汉语书注意课文的文学性。我们的整套教材包含三本书，这一本**基础汉语---中文益智宫**强调幽默易懂的风格。下一本**中级汉语 --- 中文科学园**把课文和生物、物理等自然科学相结合。第三本**高级汉语 --- 了解中国**文字优美，每一课都是很好的中文文学教材，还包括了大量的历史、文学、语言、人文地理、旅游知识。全套书越往后有越多的成语出现，能提高学生的读写和欣赏水平。全书引导学生学习更多的汉字、更多的成语，喜欢汉语、了解中国、热爱中国语言和中国文学。

　　本书每一课都有词汇表、成语讲解、问题讨论和作业练习。每课后面都专门写了"实用汉语"。这些实用汉语正是针对汉语基础、听力和口语还不够好的读者对"问候"、"商店"、"旅行"等实用场合口语的训练。所以，如果你感觉程度还不够，不妨"喧宾夺主"，先放开主课文，着重每课的"实用汉语"部分，集中补课加强对实用汉语的学习。如果你已经学会了各种实用场合的口语，请你集中精力到主课，欣赏每一课的主课文和课文的解释，提高水平更上一层楼，熟悉中国的历史和文学，学会汉语这门古老而有用的学问。

本书中有些课文是基于民间广泛流传的笑话和古代寓言。我们加上了汉语拼音、英文翻译、课文解释、词汇表和问题讨论，把它们写成汉语教材。其余的课文则是由本书作者创作的。本书的两位作者既在中国受过严格的教育，又在美国、加拿大从事教学实践多年。 这套教材适用于美国和加拿大汉语作为第二语言的课堂教学，欢迎使用者提出宝贵建议。

看五洲四海，学习中文的浪潮云水翻腾风雷激荡，越来越多的人认识到，汉语不仅仅是一门有悠久历史的古老语言，而且是当今世界各国经济交流和文化来往必不可少的重要语言工具。在西方世界普及汉语教育，此其时也。愿大家携手共进，把汉语教育的浪潮推向新的高度。

Joy Betz （美国）
常崇安 　（加拿大）

Lesson 1
Numbers and Human Beings
第一课　　人和数字

人，一个人。

手，两只手，左手、右手。

一个人有四肢：两手、两脚。

每只手有五个手指，一共十个手指。

七窍是指双眼、双耳、两个鼻孔和一张嘴。

多数人有 28 颗到 32 颗牙齿，还有千百根头发。

数字和人的关系可真密切啊！

词汇 Words

四肢	sì zhī	four limbs
手	shǒu	hand
脚	jiǎo	foot
手指	shǒu zhǐ	finger
窍	qiào	hole
双	shuāng	two, double
鼻孔	bí kǒng	nostril
嘴	zuǐ	mouth
牙齿	yá chǐ	tooth, teeth
头发	tóu fà	hair

关系	guān xì	relation
密切	mì qiè	close

语法 Grammar

在汉语中量词很多，要学习正确的用法。本文中手指用"个"，牙齿用"颗"，头发用"根"，嘴用"张"。

"五个手指"是准确的说法，但"千百根头发"是形容多，并不是一个准确的数字。形容多种多样眼花缭乱的成语"五花八门"，形容几个人一齐做某事时的成语"七手八脚"，这里的五、七和八也并非准确数字。

"28"和"32"也可以写成"二十八"和"三十二"。大于10的数通常都写成阿拉伯数字。

"Quantifier" is special in Chinese. We should pay attention to quantifiers. In this text we use "个"to count fingers, "颗"for teeth, "根" for hair and "张" to count the number of mouths.

The statement "five fingers" is an accurate numerical count, while the statement "thousands of hair" is not.

练习 Exercises

[1] 用数字 1，2，3，4，5 各造一句。

Construct five sentences and use the numbers 1, 2, 3, 4, 5 each once.

[2] 在老师的帮助下阅读下面的文字，注意其中量词的使用。

Read the following poem with help from your teacher. Pay attention to the use of different quantifiers. （青蛙 frog，眼睛 eye，腿 leg，扑通 *putong*, describing the sound when a frog jumps into a pond.）

一只青蛙一张嘴，
两个眼睛四条腿，

扑通一声跳下水。

Yī zhī qīng wān yī zhāng zuǐ,
Liǎng gè yǎn jīng sì tiáo tuǐ,
Pū tōng yī shēng tiào xià shuǐ.

两只青蛙两张嘴,
四个眼睛八条腿,
扑通扑通跳下水。

Liǎng zhī qīng wān liǎng zhāng zuǐ,
Sì gè yǎn jīng bā tiáo tuǐ,
Pū tōng pū tōng tiào xià shuǐ.

Image © Alila Sao Mai, 2012. Used under license
from Shutterstock, Inc.

实用汉语 Practical Chinese (1)
数字 Numbers

课文中用到的数字 Numbers in the text
一（1）
两、二（2）
四（4）
五（5）
七（7）
十（10）
二十八（28）
三十二（32）
千（1000）
百（100）

请大家学习数字 Learn Numbers
一、 二、 三、 四、 五、 六、 七、 八、 九、 十
yī, èr, sān, sì, wǔ, liù, qī, bā, jiǔ, shí
1   2   3   4   5   6   7   8   9   10

十一、 十二、 十三
shí yī, shí èr, shí sān
11   12   13

二十一、 二十二、 二十三
èr shí yī, èr shí èr, èr shí sān
21   22   23

练习 Exercises

[1] 把意义相同的字用线连起来
Match the numbers

11	sān shí èr	nine	九
7	shí sì	sixteen	三十二
4	èr shí yī	thirty-seven	二十六
9	shí liù	eleven	二十一
14	sān shí qī	twenty-one	四
16	èr shí liù	thirty-two	十四
21	sì	seven	七
26	shí yī	four	十一
32	qī	fourteen	三十七
37	jiǔ	twenty-six	十六

[2] 把下面的句子译为汉语并且念出来
Translate the following into Chinese and read them

I am thirteen this year.
She has three sons.
I have two brothers.
Two plus four is six.
A person has thirty-two teeth,
Ten plus three is not fourteen.

[3] 把下面的句子译为英语
Translate the following into English

她有二十五元钱。
我们一共八个人。
琳达今年三十五岁。
买四十二本书一共花了六十三元。
九只青蛙十八个眼睛、三十六条腿。

[4] 改正错误的答案
Correct the wrong answers

二十二加上九是四十
十七加上十六是二十八
三十四加上四十五是六十一
八加上九加上二十三是五十六
四、十、二十九、十八一共是八十二

[5] 继续写青蛙歌谣
在"两只青蛙两张嘴"之后再写三只、四只、五只青蛙等等。

Extend the song of frogs to three, four, five frogs, etc.

Lesson 2
The Vicious Number
第二课 数字们害怕谁

当 0, 1, 2, 3, 4, 5, 6, 7, 8, 9 这十个数字排成一队在一起玩耍时, 它们总是害怕其中的一个数字。那个数字特别凶, 它会欺负其他的数字。你知道那个数字是哪一个吗?

原来, 数字们最害怕 6, 因为人们读数时说 6、7、8, 听起来好像是 "6 欺 8"。

词汇 Words

玩耍	wán shuǎ	play
害怕	hài pà	be afraid of, fear
凶	xiōng	vicious
欺负	qī fù	bully
其他	qí tā	other
听起来	tīng qǐ lái	sounds like
好像	hǎo xiàng	seems to be, like

问题 Question

在汉语里为什么数字们害怕 6？在英语里数字们害怕谁？

In Chinese, why are the numbers afraid of the number 6?

In English, which number is the vicious number?

练习 Exercise

在网上学习一个笑话，用中文和英文讲给大家听。

Search the internet and find a joke, tell it in Chinese and in English to your friends.

实用汉语 Practical Chinese (2)
问候 Greetings

对话 Dialogue

[1]
克丽小姐，你好！
好，你也好，可伦坡先生！

Kè lì xiǎo jiě, nǐ hǎo!
Hǎo, nǐ yě hǎo, kě lún pō xiān shēng!

How are you, Miss Kelly!
I am fine, and you, Mr. Columbo?

[2]
早上好，张大哥！你上哪里去呢？
早上好，小吴。我上学校去，今天我要去教课。

Zǎo shàng hǎo, zhāng dà gē! Nǐ shàng nǎ lǐ qù ne?
Zǎo shàng hǎo, xiǎo wú! Wǒ shàng xué xiào qù, jīn tiān wǒ yào qù jiāo kè.

Good morning, brother Zhang! Where are you going?
Good morning, Xiao Wu. I am on my way to the school.
I'm teaching today.

[3]
李大姐，最近忙吗？
还好，不是太忙。你呢？
我真是太忙了，连好好休息一下的时间都没有。

9

啊，即使你很忙也请注意身体。

Lǐ dà jiě, zuì jìn máng mā?
Hái hǎo, bú shì tài máng. Nǐ ne?
Wǒ zhēn shì tài máng le, lián hǎo hǎo xiū xí yī xià de shí jiān dōu méi yǒu.
À, jí shǐ nǐ hěn máng yě qǐng zhù yì shēn tǐ.

Sister Li, have you been busy recently?
So-so, not too busy. How about you?
I've been really busy; don't even have time to rest.
Oh, please remember to take care of yourself even if you are busy.

[4]
于太太，你上街买东西吗？
小夏，我去邮局买邮票。你呢？
我去图书馆借书。我们一路走好吗？

Yú tài tài, nǐ shàng jiē mǎi dōng xī mā?
Xiǎo xià, wǒ qù yóu jú mǎi yóu piào, nǐ ne?
Wǒ qù tú shū guǎn jiè shū. wǒ mén yī qǐ zǒu hǎo mā?

Are you going shopping, Mrs. Yu?
 I'm going to the post office to buy stamps, Xiao Xia. How about you?
I'm going to the library to borrow some books. Can we go together?

[5]
下午好，哈里斯，你吃过午饭了吗？
下午好，温迪，我已经吃过了。你愿意和我去公园看看吗？
对不起，哈里斯。我还没有来得及吃午饭，今天不行了。
明天见！

10

明天见！

Xià wǔ hǎo, hǎ lǐ sī, nǐ chī guò wǔ fàn le mā?
Xià wǔ hǎo, wēn dí, wǒ yǐ jīng chī guò le. Nǐ yuàn yì hé wǒ qù gōng yuán kàn kàn mā?
Duì bú qǐ, hǎ lǐ sī, wǒ hái méi yǒu lái dé jí chī wǔ fàn, jīn tiān bù xíng le.
Míng tiān jiàn!
Míng tiān jiàn!

Good afternoon, Harris! Have you had your lunch?
Good afternoon, Wendy! I already had my lunch. Do you want to go to the park with me?
Sorry, Harris, I haven't had time for my lunch yet. I'm afraid that I can't make it today.
See you tomorrow!
See you tomorrow!

Lesson 3
It Is Not Hard to Jump High
第三课　　　跳得高不难

你相信吗？跳得比大树还高不难，你和我都能办到，不需要是超人。

学了这一课，你就会跳得比大树还要高了。

秘密在哪里呢？

[答案] 原来你只要随便一跳就行了，因为大树根本不会跳高！

词汇 Words

超人	chāo rén	superman, super girl
相信	xiāng xìn	believe
秘密	mì mì	secret
跳高	tiào gāo	high jumping
随便	suí biàn	randomly do it, casual
笑话	xiào huà	joke

问题 Question

为什么人能轻易地跳得比大树还要高呢？

Why can we easily jump higher than a tall tree?

练习 Exercise

在网上再学习一个笑话，讲给大家听。

Search the internet and find another joke, tell it to your class.

Can you jump higher than a tall tree?

你能跳得比大树还高吗？

实用汉语 Practical Chinese (3)
礼貌 Courtesy

常用语 Common phrases

您好	nín hǎo	how are you
你好	nǐ hǎo	how are you, hello
早上好	zǎo shàng hǎo	good morning
对不起	duì bù qǐ	sorry, excuse me
谢谢	xiè xiè	thank you
非常感谢	fēi cháng gǎn xiè	thank you very much
再见	zài jiàn	good bye
是我错了	shì wǒ cuò le	it's my mistake
可以吗	kě yǐ mā	may I
请	qǐng	please
太好了	tài hǎo le	excellent
没问题	méi wèn tí	no problem, it is OK
道歉	dào qiàn	apologize
我能帮帮你吗	Wǒ néng bāng bāng nǐ ma? Can I help you?	
请你帮我一下	Qǐng nǐ bāng wǒ yī xià. Can you do me a favour?	

例句 Examples

[1] 你好，王太太！
How are you, Mrs.Wang!
[2] 你好，小兰！
How are you, Xiao Lan!
[3] 对不起，你有空帮我一下吗？
Sorry, can you do me a favour?
[4] 没问题，请问我能帮你做些什么呢？

15

No problem, may I ask you what I can do for you?

[5] 请你帮我发一封信好吗？

Can you please mail a letter for me?

[6] 当然可以啦，我一定办到。

Of course, I'll certainly do it.

[7] 非常感谢！我今天实在没有时间。

Thank you very much! I really do not have time today.

[8] 不谢，小事一件。请放心。

You are welcome. That's not a problem, don't worry about it.

[9] 再见，小兰！

Good bye, Xiao Lan!

[10] 再见，王太太！

Bye! Mrs. Wang!

请你把下列句子翻译为英语
Translate the sentences into English.

[1] 刘先生，请问你有空吗？可以请你帮我做件事吗？

[2] 非常感谢您，琼斯太太。您帮了我太多了。

[3] 对不起，小李，我忘记把你的信带来给你了。

[4] 没关系，我自己去取就是了。不必说对不起。

[5] 早上好周老师，今天我可以帮你做什么吗？

请你把下列句子翻译为汉语
Translate the sentences into Chinese.

[1] Excuse me, may I ask you a question?

[2] I am sorry. I apologize for my being late.

[3] Good morning Mr. Wang, thank you for your help yesterday.

[4] Can I help you, Sir?

[5] You are very nice to me, thank you very much!

Lesson 4
The Worried Patient
第四课　求医

　　有个人嗓子疼找医生看病，医生说他是扁桃发炎，动手术把他的扁桃腺割了。后来他得了阑尾炎，找同一医生看病，医生给他把阑尾割了。不久他又病了，来找同一位医生，战战兢兢地对医生说："大夫，我好害怕哟。这次我可是得的头痛病，你会把我的头割了吗？"

词汇 Words

嗓子	sǎng zi	throat
扁桃腺	biǎn táo xiàn	tonsils
割	gē	cut off
发炎	fā yán	inflammation
手术	shǒu shù	surgery operation
阑尾	lán wěi	vermiform appendix
阑尾炎	lán wěi yán	appendicitis
头痛（头疼）	tóu tòng (tóu téng)	headache
头	tóu	head

成语 Idiom

战战兢兢　　zhàn zhàn jǐng jǐng　　trembling, fear

问题 Question

那个人第三次去见医生的时候害怕什么呢？他为什么会害怕？

When the patient went to see the doctor the third time, why was he afraid, and what was he afraid of?

读汉语并且翻译为英语
Read and translate the following into English.

[1] 今天我头痛，不能上学。

[2] 昨天我嗓子痛，可能是扁桃腺发炎了吧？

[3] 那个医生的方法很可怕哟。

[4] 布兰克医生 (Dr. Black) 是个好医生，我们都喜欢他。

[5] 我已经找那位医生三次了。

练习 Exercise

用英语和汉语自己创作一个笑话，讲给大家听。

Create and write a joke in both English and Chinese, read the joke in front of your classmates.

实用汉语 Practical Chinese (4)
打电话 Making a phone call

A
对话 Dialogue

请问，张大姐在吗？
在，请您稍等。张大姐，你的电话！

Qǐng wèn, zhāng dà jiě zài ma?
Zài, qǐng nín shāo děng. Zhāng dà jiě, nǐ de diàn huà!

May I ask you, is Mme Zhang there?
Yes, wait a minute please. Mme Zhang, your phone call!

我是张丽，请问你是哪位？
我是何清。张大姐你身体好吗？

Wǒ shì zhāng lì, qǐng wèn nǐ shì nǎ wèi?
Wǒ shì hé qīng, zhāng dà jiě nǐ shēn tǐ hǎo mā?

I am Zhangli, may I ask who is calling?
I am Heqing. How are you, Mme Zhang?

何清你好，我的身体还好。你呢？
我的身体不如以前。现在经常感觉很累。

Hé qīng nǐ hǎo, wǒ de shēn tǐ hái hǎo. nǐ ne?

Wǒ de shēn tǐ bù rú yǐ qián. Xiàn zài jīng cháng gǎn jué hěn lèi.

How are you Heqing? I am well. How about you?
I am not as strong as before. Nowadays I often feel quite tired.

小何，听得出来你声音很累。你要注意休息，别太累了。
知道了，谢谢。张大姐，你有腿脚保健方面的书吗？

Xiǎo hé, tīng dé chū lái nǐ shēng yīn hěn lèi, nǐ yào zhù yì xiū xí, bié tài lèi le.
Zhī dào lě, xiè xiè. Zhāng dà jiě, nǐ yǒu tuǐ jiǎo bǎo jiàn fāng miàn de shū mā?

Xiao He, you do sound tired. Pay attention to your health and relax more, don't work too hard.
Yes, I got it. Thanks. Mme Zhang, do you have any books on how to keep legs and feet healthy?

有的。刘老师的著作"活到老，走到老"。
太好了，我听说过她，已经 100 多岁还十分健康。

Yǒu dé. Liú lǎo shī de zhù zuó "huó dào lǎo, zǒu dào lǎo".
Tài hǎo le, wǒ tīng shuō guò tā, yǐ jīng yī bǎi duō suì hái shí fēn jiàn kāng.

Yes, I have the book "Walk, Walk, Always Walk!" by Professor Liu.
Excellent, I have heard of her. She is over 100 and still very healthy.

她过去每天都要步行 3 公里，风雨不间断地坚持了 60 年。

真是不容易。我要向她学习，每天走路上下班。

Tā guò qù měi tiān dōu yào bù xíng sānq gōng lǐ, fēng yǔ bù jiān duàn dì jiān chì le liù shí nián.

Zhēn shì bù róng yì. wǒ yào xiàng tā xué xí, měi tiān zǒu lù shàng xià bān.

She walked 3 km each day for 60 years without any interruptions.

That is unbelievable! I must learn from her. From now on I will walk to my work every day.

坚持几个月，你的身体就会大有改善。

谢谢你的吉言。那我什么时候可以到你那儿拿书呢？

Jiān chì jǐ gè yuè, nǐ de shēn tǐ jiù huì dà yǒu gǎi shàn.

Xiè xiè nǐ de jí yán. Nà wǒ shé mō shí hòu kě yǐ dào nǐ nà er ná shū ne?

Keep doing it for several months and your health will be much improved.

Thank you for your encouragement. When can I go to your place to pick up that book?

下午 4 点好不好？

好的，我 4 点到你家。再见！

Xià wǔ sì diǎn hǎo bù hǎo?

Hǎo de, wǒ sì diǎn dào nǐ jiā. Zài jiàn!

How about 4 pm today?

That's good. I will be at your home at 4 pm. Good bye!

小何，我挂电话啦，再见！
张大姐，我也挂啦，再见！

Xiǎo hé, wǒ guà diàn huà lā, zài jiàn!
Zhāng dà jiě, wǒ yě guà lā, zài jiàn!

I'm hanging up. Good bye Xiao He!
I'm also hanging up now. Good bye Mme Zhang!

Lesson 5
The Last Golden Apple
第五课 最后一个金苹果

　　贪心先生得到了三个金苹果。每吃掉一个金苹果时都可以许个愿，而这个愿望一定会实现。他先得到了两个最想要的东西。你知道他最后一个愿望是什么吗？

　　贪心先生吃掉第三个苹果的时候说：希望最后这一个苹果能给我带来数不清的有同样法力的金苹果！

词汇 Words

贪心	tān xīn	greedy
愿望	yuàn wàng	wish
许愿	xǔ yuàn	make a wish
实现	shí xiàn	become true, achieve
数不清	shǔ bù qīng	numerous, countless
法力	fǎ lì	magic power, mana

问题 Questions

[1] 那个人吃第三个金苹果的时候说了什么？
What did the man say when he ate the last golden apple?
[2] 为什么称他为"贪心先生"？
Why do we call him "Mr. Greed"?

读汉语并且翻译为英语
Read and translate into English

[1] 我很喜欢吃苹果。
[2] 要是我能得到那个金苹果就好了。
[3] 贪心先生很聪明啊，结果比他要个别的东西要好。
[4] 我有时候也贪心，很想吃很多好饭菜。
[5] 不知道那位贪心先生前两个愿望是什么？

翻译为汉语并且读出来
Translate into Chinese and read

[1] I am not a "Mr. (Ms) Greed"
[2] I wish I could get ten golden apples, or no! I want eleven!
[3] Yesterday I ate some golden apples but none gave me any magic powers.
[4] Being greedy may not be bad for a person; he or she may be motivated to work harder.
[5] I like this story; I like the golden apples in this story.
[6] I want to buy golden apples tomorrow, better the kind with magic power.

练习 Exercise

写一篇汉语短文，描述三个金苹果的故事。编出第一、第二、第三个金苹果帮助那人各完成了什么心愿，故事的结局又会是怎样。

Write a short story in Chinese about the three golden apples. Create your story so that readers know what the person got from his first, second, and third wish, and what the end of the story was.

实用汉语 Practical Chinese (5)
童年 Childhood

课文

我的童年过得非常愉快。奶奶和爷爷经常带我去公园玩，爸爸妈妈平时很忙，但是星期天总会陪我一起去看电影或者上少年宫学习滑冰和游泳。我从小就喜欢读书，很小的时候就读了不少童话、神话和民间故事书。我不光看儿童卡通电视，还喜欢看动物世界、科学发现和其它有趣的电视节目。有一次我走路不小心摔倒了，很想哭，可是想起故事里的小英雄，就告诉自己要坚强，结果我就没有哭。

Text

I had a very happy childhood. When I was young my grandma and grandpa often brought me to the park to play. Although my mother and father were busy on weekdays, they always took me to watch movies, or to learn swimming and skating at the Center for Kids on weekends. I loved reading. From very young I started reading fairy tales, myths, and folk story books. I not only watched children's catoons on TV, but also liked watching programs like "The Animal World", the Discovery Channel, Scientific Invention, and others. One day I fell on the road and almost cried. But then I remembered the heroes in my story books, so I told myself to be strong and stood up without tears.

词汇 Words

童年	tóng nián	childhood
电影	diàn yǐng	movie
少年宫	shào nián gōng	Center for Kids
滑冰	huá bīng	skate
游泳	yóu yǒng	swim
童话	tóng huà	fairy tales
神话	shén huà	myths
民间故事	mín jiān gù shì	folk stories
卡通	kě tōng	cartoon
动物世界	dòng wù shì iè	The Animal's World
电视节目	diàn shì jié mù	TV programs
摔倒	shuāi dǎo	fall on the ground
坚强	jiān qiáng	strong
哭	kū	cry

练习 Exercise

写 1 段儿时的回忆。

Xiě yī duàn ér shí de huí yì.

Write an article about your own childhood.

问题 Questions

[1] 你小时候喜欢看什么电视节目，为什么呢？

Nǐ xiǎo shí hòu xǐ huān kàn shé mō diàn shì jié mù, wèi shé mō ne?

When you were young, what TV programs did you like to watch? Why?

[2] 什么样的儿童生活是有意义的？

Shé mō yàng de ér tóng shēng huó shì yǒu yì yì de?

27

What kind of childhood do you think is meaningful?

[3] 你小时候读过些什么书？请举例说明。

Nǐ xiǎo shí hòu dú guò xiē shé mō shū? qǐng jǔ lì shuō míng.

What kind of books did you read when you were young? Please give examples.

Lesson 6
Smart Girl Qiaoqiao
第六课 聪明的巧巧

　　巧巧的父母在很远的外地工作，巧巧和奶奶一起生活。有一天巧巧顽皮，奶奶提笔写信给在外地的巧巧的爸爸妈妈，信上写道："巧巧不乖"。聪明伶俐的巧巧看到了，微微一笑，提笔改成"巧巧还乖"。轻易地就化解了这场"危机"。大家知道了都说巧巧真聪明。

　　原始森林的深处住着一位老智慧伯伯。有一天他给巧巧出了一道难题：给"菜、竞、西、云、利"这5个字，每字添上一笔，变成其它的5个字。

　　巧巧想来想去，把5个字都想出来了。原来，上面那些字只要添上一笔就能变成另一个字，"菊、竟、酉、去、刹"汉语真有意思！

　　还有一些字，例如"曰"添上一笔，可以变成不止一个字（田、申、甲、由、电），这里面的学问可就更多啦。

29

词汇 Words

顽皮	wán pí	naughty
乖	guāi	cute
聪明	cōng míng	smart
危机	wēi jī	crisis
伶俐	líng lì	clever, act quickly
轻易	qīng yì	easily
化解	huà jiě	resolve
原始森林	yuán shǐ sēn lín	primeval forest
智慧	zhì huì	wisdom
学问	xué wèn	knowledge

Workers working in a primeval forest
原始森林的林区工人

成语 Idiom

聪明伶俐　　　cōng míng líng lì　　　cute and smart

问题 Question

巧巧是怎样化解了"危机"的呢？
How did she resolve the "crisis"?

讲解 Explanation

危机本来是指很严重的事，放在引号里"危机"就成了夸张和比喻，是一种轻松愉快的说法。

Crisis could be very serious; however in quotes here "crisis" means something exaggerated and not so serious.

曰不是日。曰（yuē）是古代汉语中的"说"，而日（rì）是太阳的意思，一日就是一天。

曰 (yuē) is not 日(rì). 曰 means "to say" in ancient Chinese, and 日 means a day or the sun.

练习 Exercises

[1] 有许多汉字可以轻易地加上一划变成另一个汉字。请你在"田"字上加上一笔，变成另外的字。做法越多越好。

Many Chinese characters can be converted to another character by adding just one stroke. Try this to the word "田". Try as many ways as possible.

[2] 今天许多时候我们用打电话或者发电子邮件的方式和人交流，用笔写的信越来越少见也越来越宝贵。建议你收集可以找到的前人的信件加以收藏。另外，请你给一位家人用笔和纸写一封家信。

31

Nowadays we call or email others instead of writing a letter on paper and sending it via regular mail. Hand written letters are becoming rare and more precious. Write a letter by pen and paper to a family member.

[3] 查字典弄懂"竞"和"竟"的区别。

Understand the difference between "竞" and "竟". You may use a dictionary if needed.

[4] 再举出几个字，如果添加一笔可以变成其它的字。如果能变成不止 1 个新字更好。

List more examples similar to the ones in this story (by adding one stroke, we can change a character into another, or even several other new characters).

实用汉语 Practical Chinese (6)
家庭 Family

A.
基本词汇 Basic words

爸爸	bà ba	father
妈妈	mā ma	mother
兄弟	xiōng dì	brother
姐妹	jiě mèi	sister
爷爷	yé ye	grandfather
奶奶	nǎi nai	grandmother
儿子	ér zǐ	son
女儿	nǚ ér	daughter

B.
更多的词汇 More words

英语的同一个称呼词在汉语中可以细分为几个词。请你和老师、同学讨论，明白这些词在汉语中的细致含义区别。

Aunt: 姑姑、姨、舅母

Uncle: 伯伯、叔叔、舅舅

Grandmother (grandma): 奶奶、姥姥

Grandfather (grandpa): 爷爷、姥爷

哥哥、弟弟在英语中可以统称为 brother，姐姐、妹妹可以统称为 sister。

（还有更多的词，仅举一例：嫂嫂、弟妹，在汉语中有区别，但在英语中都称为 sister-in-law）

33

C.
词汇连接
Match the words with the same meaning.

爸爸	jiù jiu	son
奶奶	mā ma	niece
孙儿	zhí ér	granddaughter
姐姐	zhí nǚ	father
爷爷	nǎi nai	sister (elder)
侄女	nǚ ér	grandfather
舅舅	shū shu	mother
叔叔	lǎo lao	grandmother
伯伯	sūn nǚ	daughter
姥姥	sūn ér	nephew
妹妹	mèi mei	grandson
妈妈	jiě jie	uncle
孙女	yé ye	grandmother
侄儿	bó bo	uncle
女儿	ér zǐ	uncle
儿子	bà ba	sister (younger)

Lesson 7
Cry and Laugh
第七课 哭与笑

托尼很喜欢学习汉语。他在纸上写了两个很大的字，一个是"哭"，一个是"笑"。

他越看越觉得，哭字真的很像一个人在哭，那一点画龙点睛就是眼睛里流下的眼泪。而笑字又真的很像一个人在笑，上面是一双笑眼，下面又刻画出那张笑脸。他对玛丽老师说：古时候的人造字真的造得很神奇，妙得很。

玛丽老师说：汉字是从象形的符号发展起来的。造得神奇的例子多不胜举。"田"字像一方方的土地，"飞"字真的好像要飞腾，"雨"字里边的四点就是天上落下的雨点。三人为"众"，三木为"森"，太形象了。我们要爱汉语、学汉语，努力把汉语记在心里。

词汇 Words

眼睛	yǎn jīng	eyes
眼泪	yǎn lèi	tears
像	xiàng	look like
刻画	kè huà	carve, describe
象形	xiàng xíng	pictographic
符号	fú hào	symbol
飞腾	fēi téng	fly to the sky
形象	xíng xiàng	vivid, like the original

成语 Idioms

画龙点睛	huà lóng diǎn jīng	the final key step
多不胜举	duō bú shèng jǔ	many, countless

问题 Questions

[1] 古时候的人是按照怎样的规律造汉字的？

How did Chinese ancestors create the characters?

[2] 和英语的造词方法对比一下，有哪些不同？各有什么好处？

Compare English with Chinese. What are the differences between these two languages? What are the advantages for each?

练习 Exercises

[1] 再举出几个汉字非常形象的例子。

Give more examples of Chinese words that look vivid as the object they describe.

[2] 用"画龙点睛"造句。

Construct a sentence using the idiom "画龙点睛".

[3] Write"哭" and "笑" on paper, look at them closely, and see if you see what Tony saw.

实用汉语 Practical Chinese (7)
餐馆 In a restaurant

A.
对话 Dialogue

客人您好，请问您需要些什么呢？
我想点一份烤鸡、一盘色拉。
您需要什么饮料吗？
你们这里有什么饮料呢？
我们供应可口可乐、雪碧、牛奶和咖啡。
我要一杯雪碧。
那好，烤鸡 5 分钟之内就会准备完毕。
谢谢！
不用谢。

Kè rén nín hǎo, qǐng wèn nín xū yào xiē shé mō ne?
Wǒ xiǎng diǎn yī fèn kǎo jī, yī pán sè lā.
Nín xū yào shé mō yǐn liào mā?
Nǐ mén zhè lǐ yǒu shé mō yǐn liào ne?
Wǒ mén gòng yīng kě kǒu kě lè, xuě bì, niú nǎi hé kā fēi.
Wǒ yào yī bēi xuě bì.
Nà hǎo, kǎo jī wǔ fēn zhōng zhī nèi jiù huì zhǔn bèi wán bì.
Xiè xiè!
Bù yòng xiè.

How are you Mme (Sir), may I ask you what I can do for you?

I want to order fried chicken and a salad.
Do you need something to drink?
What kind of drinks do you have?
We have Coke Cola, Sprite, milk and coffee.

Then I would like to have a Sprite please.
Good, the chicken will be ready in five minutes.
Thank you!
You are welcome!

B.
用中文写一段话，描述在一个餐馆发生的事。
Write a paragraph in Chinese to describe an event in a restaurant.

Lesson 8
The Rule Is Wrong
第八课 规则错了

妈妈给小妮可讲解交通规则，教妮可要听从警察叔叔阿姨的指挥，沿马路右边走，要从人行道过马路，还说人人都应该这样做。

小妮可忽然说：妈妈，这里边有一条规则错了！

妈妈问：哪一条规则不对了呢？

妮可说：要是人人都沿马路的右边走，路的左边没有人走怎么办呢？

词汇 Words

规则	guī zé	rules
交通	jiāo tōng	traffic
讲解	jiǎng jiě	explain
警察	jǐng chá	police
指挥	zhǐ huī	command

马路	mǎ lù	street
人行道	rén xíng dào	side walk
忽然	hū rán	suddenly

问题 Question
想一想，妈妈会怎样回答妮可的疑问。
How would the mother answer Nicole's question?

练习 Exercise
再想出几条交通规则来。
List a few more traffic rules.

知识 Knowledge
并不是每个国家的交通规则像美国、加拿大、中国一样，规定行人沿马路的右方人行道走。在有些地方，交通规则的规定是相反的，人们要沿路的左方走，汽车也沿马路的左边开驶。试举出一个例子。

Not every country designs traffic rules in the same way as in the United States, Canada and China. Some other countries require cars to use the left lane and pedestrians to walk on the left side of the street. Find one such country as an example.

实用汉语 Practical Chinese (8)
生日 Birthday

Image © Elena Elisseeva, 2012. Used under license
from Shutterstock, Inc.

A.
词汇 Words

生日	shēng rì	birthday
蛋糕	dàn gāo	cake
唱生日歌	chàng shēng rì gē	
	singing the song "*Happy Birthday to You*"	
聚会	jù huì	party
礼物盒	lǐ wù hé	gift box
卡片	kǎ piàn	cards
音乐会	yīn yuè huì	concert

票	piào	ticket
玩具	wán jù	toy
书籍	shū jí	book
手机	shǒu jī	cellular phone
旅行	lǚ xíng	travel
出国	chū guó	go abroad
庆祝	qìng zhù	celebrate, celebration
购买	gòu mǎi	buy, purchase
赠送	zèng sòng	present, send as a gift
舞会	wǔ huì	dancing party
花束	huā shù	bouquet

B.
课文 Text

姐妹们商议如何给妈妈过 60 岁的生日。

玲玲说："我要给妈妈送庆祝生日的礼物盒，里边放玩具、书籍和卡片。"

雅云说："还要为妈妈购买生日蛋糕，开个大聚会，唱生日歌、办舞会。"

爱米说："我要赠送妈妈音乐会的票，还要送她生日花束。"

温迪说："我要送妈妈出国旅游，还要送她一个新手机。"

爸爸妈妈听了都很高兴。

C.
读上面的课文
Read the above text.

D.
把上面的课文译为英语
Translate the above text into English.

Lesson 9
An Impatient Person
第九课 心急的人

　　从前有个人心很急，办什么事都着急忙慌。有一次他到面馆吃面。他的帽子比较大，戴在头上有点松垮。他低头喝面汤帽沿就落在碗里沾着汤。他用手把帽沿推上去又低头喝汤，结果帽子又一次落下来，帽沿又挨着汤了。

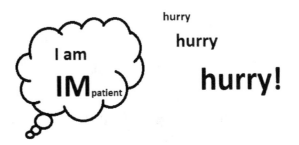

　　这个人于是大怒，把帽子一把抓下来，用劲把整个帽子塞进汤碗，说："我让你吃、让你吃！你就喝个饱吧，我不吃了！我不吃了！"

词汇 Words

面馆	miàn guǎn	noodle restaurant
松垮	sōng kuǎ	loose
帽子	mào zǐ	hat
帽沿	mào yán	brim of a hat
汤	tāng	soup
大怒	dà nù	very angry
整个	zhěng gè	whole
塞进	sāi jìn	stuffed into
汤碗	tāng wǎn	the soup bowl

成语 Idiom
着急忙慌　　zháo jí máng huāng　　panic, hurry

问题 Questions
[1] 和 "着急忙慌" 相反的成语是什么？
Which idiom has the opposite meaning to the idiom "着急忙慌"？
[2] 这个故事告诉我们什么道理？
What lesson can we learn from this story?

练习 Exercises
[1] 把这个故事用中文讲给全班听。
Tell the class this story in Chinese.
[2] 把这个故事用英文讲给你家里人听，他们笑了吗？
Tell your family this story in English, did they laugh?

实用汉语 Practical Chinese (9)
约会 Arranging appointments

A.
句型
Model sentences

[1] 汤姆让我告诉你，他今天下午 4 点有个重要约会，不能来学校。

Tāng mǔ ràng wǒ gào sù nǐ, tā jīn tiān xià wǔ sì diǎn yǒu gè zhòng yào yuē huì, bù néng lái xué xiào.

Tom wants me to tell you that he has an important appointment at 4 pm this afternoon so he cannot be at the school.

[2] 我们下一次的约会是下周星期三吗？

wǒ mén xià yī cì de yuē huì shì xià zhōu xīng qī sān mā?

Is our next appointment on Wednesday the following week?

[3] 小王，我们的约会时间改了，不在明天早上 9 点，而是在后天早上同一时间。

Xiǎo wáng, wǒ mén de yuē huì shí jiān gǎi le, bú zài míng tián zǎo shàng jiǔ diǎn, ér shì zài hòu tiān zǎo shàng tóng yī shí jiān.

Xiao Wang, our appointment has been changed; it will be 9 AM the day after tomorrow, not 9 o'clock tomorrow morning.

[4] 朋友们，我们下次聚会的地点将是在人民公园的荷花池边上。

Péng yǒu mén, wǒ mén xià cì jù huì de dì diǎn jiāng shì zài rén mín gōng yuán de hé huā chí biān shàng.

My friends, the location of our next party will be at the lotus flower pond of the People's Park.

[5] 对不起，我不能赴约，因为我先生（我太太）病了。

Duì bù qǐ, wǒ bù néng fù yuē, yīn wéi wǒ xiān shēng (wǒ tài tài) bìng le.

Sorry I cannot keep that appointment because my husband (wife) is sick.

[6] 请问，我可以约个时间找胡医生看病吗？

Qǐng wèn, wǒ kě yǐ yuē gè shí jiān zhǎo hú yī shēng kàn bìng mā?

May I make an appointment to see Dr. Hu?

[7] 海伦，您的约会时间是星期一的早晨 8 点 30 分，在院长办公室。请准时到。

Hǎi lún, nǐ de yuē huì shí jiān shì xīng qī yī de zǎo chén bā diǎn sān shí fēn, zài yuàn zhǎng bàn gōng shì. Qǐng zhǔn shí dào.

Helen, your appointment will be at 8:30 AM next Monday, in the office of the director. Please come on time.

B.
英译汉
Translate the following into Chinese.

[1] May I make an appointment with Dr. Thomas?

[2] I can go anytime. Please feel free to arrange an appointment for me. Thank you!

[3] This week I am busy. Please change my appointment to the following week.

[4] I have two appointments at the same time. I can only go for one.

[5] Mr. Zhang, the doctor wants to see you at 10 AM tomorrow. Is that OK?

C.
汉译英
Translate the following into English.

[1] 皮特，您今天下午 4 点和王经理 (Manager Wang) 有个约会。

[2] 小李，可以告诉我下周的约会时间和地点吗？

[3] 请大家记住约会的时间，不要迟到，谢谢。

[4] 今后我们每周的约会都要换一个不同的地方。

[5] 经理先生，您明天的约会时间是早上 9 点，在东方饭店 302 室。

D.
对号入座
Match the words in the three columns.

10 PM	忙	dì diǎn
Wednesday	约会	wàng jì le
10 AM	晚上 10 点	xīng qī sān
location	早上 10 点	máng
on time	准时	wǎn shàng shí diǎn
busy	星期三	zhǔn shí
forgot	地点	zǎo shàng shí diǎn
appointment	忘记了	yuē huì

Lesson 10
Two Humorous Short Stories
第十课 幽默二则

坐车

有个人要乘火车到外地去。坐慢车比较便宜，但是要多花时间。坐快车可以节约时间但是票价自然贵一些。他说：太不合理啦，多出钱理应多坐车，我多出了钱怎么反而少坐车几个小时？真不划算！

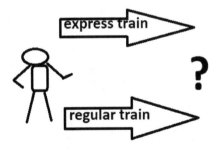

今天怎么啦？

兰兰所在的教室里正在进行一次考试。大多数人都端坐在座位上，聚精会神地思考，教室里非常安静。可是，居然有人在东张西望、从教室的一处走到另一处，还看别人写的是什么。这个班的纪律本来还不错的，今天怎么啦？

词汇 Words

幽默	yōu mò	humor, humorous
慢车	màn chē	regular (slow) train
快车	kuài chē	express train
便宜	pián yí	cheap
节约	jié yuē	save
票价	piào jià	ticket price
自然	zì rán	naturally
贵	guì	expensive
合理	hé lǐ	reasonable
理应	lǐ yīng	should
划算	huá suàn	cost effective
教室	jiào shì	classroom
考试	kǎo shì	exam
大多数	dà duō shù	most
端坐	duān zuò	sit straight
座位	zuò wèi	seat
思考	sī kǎo	thinking
安静	ān jìng	quiet
居然	jū rán	however, still
别人	bié rén	others
纪律	jì lù	discipline

不错	bú cuò	not bad

成语 Idioms：

聚精会神	jù jīng huì shén	concentrate
东张西望	dōng zhāng xī wàng	look around

问题 Questions：

[1] 是谁在东张西望呢？

Who was looking around?

[2] 你认为多花钱反而坐车时间少合理吗？

Do you agree that it is reasonable to pay more but sit in the train for less time?

练习 Exercises

[1] 请你用"居然"造一个句。

Please construct a sentence using the word "居然"。

[2] 用中文写 1 篇 100 字以内的短文，记叙今天你所在的课堂里发生的事情。

Write an article in Chinese about what happened in your classroom today using less than 100 Chinese characters.

（本课答案：原来是老师，她需要走来走去、关心每一位同学。）

实用汉语 Practical Chinese (10)
价格 Prices

A 汉译英 Translate into English

[1] 这种肉多少钱一公斤？

[2] 请问这里卖 3 元 1 公斤的桔子吗？

[3] 如果 1 公斤牛肉卖 40 元，那 10 元就能买到 250 克牛肉。

[4] 你这里还有 9 元 0.5 公斤的鸡蛋吗？对不起，卖完了。明天再来吧。

[5] 这本书的价格是 7 元，现在只卖 6 元，你能节省 1 元。

[6] 好消息！书店在卖减价的好书。

词汇 Words

肉	ròu	meat
桔子	jú zǐ	orange
公斤	gōng jīn	kilogram
钱	qián	money
多少钱	duō shǎo qián	how much
牛肉	niú ròu	beef
克	kè	gram
鸡蛋	jī dàn	egg
买	mǎi	buy
卖	mài	sell
卖完了	mài wán le	sold out
书	shū	book
价格	jià gé	price
贵	guì	expensive

便宜	pián yì	cheap
节省	jié shěng	save
消息	xiāo xī	news
减价	jiǎn jià	discount

B 英译汉 Translate into Chinese

[1] What is the price for this kind of orange?

[2] I only have ten dollars. Is that enough for me to buy 1 kilogram of beef?

[3] Two eggs together cost 7.8 Chinese *Yuan*. How much would three eggs cost?

[4] May I ask you the price for this bag of rice?

[5] If you do not buy now, the price may go higher tomorrow.

C 词汇配对 Match the words

价格	duō shǎo	buy
公斤	guì	cheap
便宜	mài	price
卖	mǎi	gram
克	jià gé	how much
贵	gōng jīn	kilogram
买	pián yì	expensive
多少	kè	sell

Lesson 11
What Grows Smaller and Smaller
第十一课 什么东西越长越小

儿童们一天天长大，身体逐渐长高。可是，世界是复杂多样的，今天老师问：有没有什么是越长越小、越长越矮的呢？（不但有，而且就在我们的身边，就在我们每日的生活中。）

杰米猜到了答案：铅笔越长越矮。

辛迪也猜到了答案：橡皮擦越活越小。

老师又提出一个问题：假如 1 支铅笔每天用去 1 半的长度，在哪一天它的长度是今天的 8 倍？

答案是什么呢？请讨论。

词汇 Words

逐渐	zhú jiàn	gradually, step by step
矮	ǎi	short, dwarf
铅笔	qiān bǐ	pencil
橡皮擦	xiàng pí cā	eraser
长度	cháng dù	length
答案	dá àn	answer
讨论	tǎo lùn	discuss

成语 Idioms

复杂多样	fù zá duō yàng	complex, various

Why am I growing smaller and smaller?

练习 Exercises

[1] 请你想出书上没有写的三个越长越小的例子.

Please list three examples of your own where the length or volume is decreasing with time.

[2] 如果有个小神仙长得很快，每天都是上一天高度的 2 倍，这样一直长到 40 天就不再变化了。那么哪一天他的高度是他 1 岁时的四分之一？

Assume a genius grows very fast; her size is doubled everyday until she is 40 days old. On which day is her size ¼ as her size when she was one year old?

[3] 如果有一根米尺，每天长度缩短为前一天的一半，不停地按这个规律缩短下去，最后会缩短成长度为零吗？什么是“最后”的结果呢？

If a meter stick is halved everyday, will it become zero in length at the end? What would be the "final length"?

实用汉语 Practical Chinese (11)
交通 Traffic

A 词汇 Words

汽车	qì chē	car
火车	huǒ chē	train
轮船	lún chuán	ship
巴士	bā shì	bus
飞机	fēi jī	airplane
步行	bù xíng	walk
单程	dān chéng	one way
来回、往返	lái huí, wǎng fǎn	round trip
票	piào	ticket
火车站	huǒ chē zhàn	railway station
巴士站	bā shì zhàn	bus stop
码头	mǎ tóu	pier, dock
机场	jī chǎng	airport

B 句型 Model sentences

[1] 我从北京到上海坐飞机要 2 小时。
Wǒ cóng běi jīng dào shàng hǎi zuò fēi jī yào èr xiǎo shí.
It takes me 2 hours to fly from Beijing to Shanghai.

[2] 巴士比步行快，火车比汽车快，飞机最快。
Bā shì bǐ bù xíng kuài, huǒ chē bǐ qì chē kuài, fēi jī zuì kuài.
Bus moves faster than walking; a train moves faster than a car; and airplanes move the fastest.

[3] 火车站有很多人，我需要排队 1 个小时才能买到票。

Huǒ chē zhàn yǒu hěn duō rén, wǒ xū yào pái duì yī gè xiǎo shí cái néng mǎi dào piào.

There are too many people in the railway station. I need to stand in line for an hour just to buy a ticket.

[4] 从北京到成都的往返飞机票价是 2000 元。

Cóng běi jīng dào chéng dū de wǎng fǎn jī piào jià shì èr qiān yuán.

Each round trip airplane ticket between Beijing and Chengdu costs 2000 Chinese *Yuan*.

[5] 请问你知道火车站在哪里吗？可不可以乘巴士前往？

Qǐng wèn nǐ zhī dào huǒ chē zhàn zài nǎ lǐ ma? Kě bù kě yǐ chéng bā shì qián wǎng?

May I ask you where the railway station is? Can I take the bus to get there?

C 用汉语回答 Answer in Chinese

[1] 请问飞机场在哪里？
[2] 去上海的单程火车票多少钱？
[3] 下一个巴士站是哪里？
[4] 火车和汽车哪个更快呢？
[5] 我有 800 元，够买 1 张去上海的火车票吗？
[6] Where is the train station of our city?
[7] Can you please tell me the price of a train ticket from here to Chengdu?
[8] Is the plane ticket more expensive than the train ticket?
[9] May I ask you the price of an airplane ticket to fly from here to Shanghai?
[10] Why is the bus not coming? I have been waiting at this bus stop for a long time.

D 读下面的词并译为英语，再想出几个类似的词来。

Read and translate the following words into English. List more words with similar structures.

火车
汽车
三轮车
人力车
马车
牛车
电车

Lesson 12
An Endless Story
第十二课 讲不完的故事

科学家法布尔讲过 1 个故事：

小蟋蟀和小蚂蚁是好朋友。他们来到一条冻了冰的小河沟前，小蟋蟀一蹦就跳过去了，小蚂蚁学着一蹦，却把腿摔断了。

小蟋蟀就说："冰啊冰，你是强者，强者不应该欺负弱者。你不应该把我的朋友小蚂蚁的腿摔断了。"

冰说："我不是强者。太阳出来就会把我晒化了。"

小蟋蟀就说："太阳啊太阳，你是强者，强者不应该欺负弱者。你不应该把冰晒化了，冰不该把我的朋友小蚂蚁的腿摔断了。"

太阳说："我不是强者。云过来就会把我遮住了。"

小蟋蟀就说："云啊云，你是强者，强者不应该欺负弱者。你不应该把太阳档住了，太阳不应该把冰晒化了，冰不应该把我的朋友小蚂蚁的腿摔断了。"

你能把这个故事接着讲下去吗？

词汇 Words

蟋蟀	xī shuài	cricket
蚂蚁	mǎ yǐ	ant
冻了冰	dòng le bīng	frozen
河沟	hé gōu	creek
蹦	bèng	jump
摔断	shuāi duàn	break, broken
强者	qiáng zhě	strong one
弱者	ruò zhě	weak one
欺负	qī fù	bully
应该	yīng gāi	should
晒化	shài huà	melt
遮住	zhē zhù	shield, block

法布尔(fǎ bù ěr)，法国昆虫学家和作家。
Jean-Henri Fabre (1823-1915), French entomologist and author.

练习 Exercises

[1] 请你把这个故事继续编下去，至少 3 步，写成汉语并且朗读之。

Continue this story for at least three more steps, write your part in Chinese and read it out loudly.

[2] 这个故事说明了什么道理呢？
What is the lesson that this story tells us?

[3] 你能另外编一个不同的没完没了的故事吗？
Can you create a new endless story?

民歌　强和弱　A folk song

有一首民歌唱道：

> 困难像弹簧
> 看你强不强
> 你强它就弱
> 你弱它就强

讨论这首民歌的含义。
Discuss the meaning of this folk song.
(困难 difficulty, 弹簧 spring)

实用汉语 Practical Chinese (12)
书店 Bookstore

课文 Text：

啊，这个书店的书真多，各种各样的书都有。

马克喜欢文学书，埃米喜欢科学书，汉斯喜欢体育题材的书，每个人都找到了心爱的书籍。

帕蒂是这个书店的工作人员，她热心地帮助顾客挑选书籍，还仔细把每本书包好。大家都感谢帕蒂。

保罗又喜欢文学又热爱科学，帕蒂就把大科学家、大文学家法布尔的著名作品"科学的故事"和"昆虫记"介绍给他，他高高兴兴地买了这两本书回家。

注 Notes

［1］科学的故事，法布尔著； The Stories of Science, by J-H Fabre

［2］昆虫记，法布尔著；The Records about Insects, by J-H Fabre

练习 Exercises

［1］用成语"各种各样"和"高高兴兴"各造一句。
Construct Chinese sentences using the idiom "各种各样" and the idiom "高高兴兴" respectively.

［2］写1篇关于你常去的书店的小故事。

Write a short article in Chinese about your favorite bookstore and your friends.

[3] 这篇短文写了 5 个人以及法布尔，说说每个人的事。

This short article has 5 characters plus the book author Fabre. Describe each of them, what did each of them do?

Lesson 13
Trouble With Bikes
第十三课 自行车的烦恼

小彼得有一辆自行车。有一天他听到自己的自行车和同学尼娜的自行车在互相抱怨。

彼得的自行车说："彼得骑在我身上，用脚拼命地踩我。刹车的时候把我的皮肤夹得好痛好痛，可他还在座位上唱歌。他自己吃好饭，却只给我的肚子里装空气。"

尼娜的自行车说："我从生下来就没有一天天地长大过。我的小主人骑我去看电影，把我留在外面。她还要锁上我怕我逃走。其实我们虽然名叫自行车，却是根本不会'自行'的。"

词汇 Words

自行车	zì xíng chē	bicycle, bike
烦恼	fán nǎo	trouble

抱怨	bào yuàn	complain
拼命	pīn mìng	desperately
踩	cǎi	step on
刹车	shā chē	apply brake
皮肤	pí fū	skin
夹	jiā	squeeze
座位	zuò wèi	seat
唱歌	chàng gē	singing
肚子	dù zǐ	stomach
电影	diàn yǐng	movie
留	liú	remain, stay
锁	suǒ	lock
逃走	táo zǒu	escape, run out
其实	qí shí	indeed, actually
自行	zì xíng	moving by itself

问题 Questions

[1] 这一课的风格是什么？有意思吗？

What is the writing style of this story? Do you find it interesting?

[2] 你觉得"自行车"这个名称合适不合适？

Do you think the name "自行车" is fitting?

练习 Exercise：

背诵这篇课文，然后把故事讲给家人和朋友们听。

Recite the text, tell the story to your family or friends.

实用汉语 Practical Chinese (13)
学校 School

A. 句型 Model sentences

[1] 现在开始上课，早上好！
Xiàn zài kāi shǐ shàng kè, zǎo shàng hǎo!
It's time to begin the lesson. Good morning!

[2] 请翻到课本的第二十七页。
Qǐng fān dào kè běn de dì èr shí qī yè
Please turn the textbook to page 27.

[3] 你明白我讲的吗？
Nǐ míng bái wǒ jiǎng de mā?
Do you understand what I am saying?

[4] 请跟着我读。
Qǐng gēn zháo wǒ dú
Please read with me.

[5] 请安静！
Qǐng ān jìng!
Please be quiet!

[6] 今天我们学习第十一课，"如何写诗"。
Jīn tiān wǒ mén xué xí dì shí yī kè "rú hé xiě shī"
Today we are going to learn lesson 11, "how to write a poem".

[7] 下课了，同学们再见！老师再见！
Xià kè le, tóng xué mén zài jiàn! lǎo shī zài jiàn!
It is time to end our lesson. Good bye students! Goodbye teacher!

71

B. 英译汉 Translate the following into Chinese.

[1] Please turn to page 54, thank you!
[2] This is a Chinese class. Today we will learn lesson 17.
[3] It is time for me to end this lesson and go home now.
[4] Please follow me, do you understand?
[5] I must go. Good bye students!

C. 汉译英 Translate the following into English

[1] 今天星期五，我们学习第十九课"渔夫和大海的故事"。（渔夫 fisherman, 大海 ocean, sea）
[2] 上课了，同学们好！老师好！
[3] 请跟我读，谢谢！
[4] 请安静！请翻到课本第 36 页。
[5] 明白我讲的了吗？好，下课，再见！

D.对话 Dialogue

[1]
小刚：老师好！
Xiǎo Gang: Lǎo shī hǎo!
Xiao Gang: Good morning teacher!

老师：小刚好！请打开书翻到第 9 页。
Lǎo shī: Xiǎo Gang hǎo! Qǐng dǎ kāi shū fān dào dì jiǔ yè.
Teacher: Good morning Xiao Gang! Please open the book and turn to page 9.

小刚：好的。
Xiǎo Gang: Hǎo de
Xiao Gang: OK.

老师：请安静。跟着我读，谢谢！

Lǎo shī: Qǐng ān jìng. Gēn zháo wǒ dú, xiè xiè!

Teacher: Be quiet please. Read with me, thank you!

小刚：下课了，老师明天再见！

Xiǎo Gāng: Xià kè le, lǎo shī míng tiān zài jiàn!

Xiao Gang: This lesson is over. See you tomorrow teacher!

老师：大家明天再见！

Lǎo shī: Dà jiā míng tiān zài jiàn!

Teacher: See all of you tomorrow!

[2]

金子：老师好！银子和我有问题要问老师。

Jīn Zǐ: Lǎo shī hǎo! Yín Zǐ hé wǒ yǒu wèn tí yào wèn lǎo

shī

Jin Zi: How are you teacher! Yin Zi and I have some questions to ask you.

老师：请问。

Lǎo shī: Qǐng wèn

Teacher: Please ask.

银子：老师，课本里说诸葛亮是个很聪明的人。中国历史上有秦汉唐宋元明清，请问孔明先生是哪个朝代的人呢？

Yín Zǐ: Lǎo shī, kè běn lǐ shuó Zhū gě Liàng shì gè hěn cōng míng de rén. Zhōng guó lì shǐ shàng yǒu qín hàn táng sòng yuán míng qīng, qǐng wèn Kǒng Míng xiān shēng shì nǎ gè cháo dài de rén ne?

Yin Zi: Teacher, our textbook says that Zhuge Liang was a very intelligent person. We know that in Chinese history there were dynasties such as Qin, Han, Tang, Song, Yuan, Ming and Qing. May we ask you which dynasty is Mr. Kong Ming (that is, Mr. Zhuge Liang) from?

老师：孔明生活在汉代末期的三国时代。

Lǎo shī: Kǒng Míng shēng huó zài hàn dài mò qī de sān guó shí dài

Teacher: Kong Ming lived at the end of the Han dynasty, the so called "Three-Kingdoms Era".

金子: 谢谢老师!

Jīn Zǐ: Xiè xiè lǎo shī

Jin Zi: Thank you, teacher!

Lesson 14
The Chonghua Newspaper
第十四课 重华报的故事

　　雪儿和姐姐冰儿生活在北美，她们都在上中文学校。她们自办了一份手写的中文小报"重华报"，每周出一期，贴在家里让爸爸妈妈和来玩的小朋友们看。

　　重华报内容丰富，有"新诗"、"古人诗词选"、"哈哈笑"、"小小画"、"儿童乐园"、"猜一猜"、"谜语会"、"一周评论"、"妙语佳话"、"新闻短波"、"知识窗"、"天气情况"、"信息"、"漫画"、"动脑筋"等等。全部文字由姐妹俩编写，爸爸妈妈的投稿也要经雪儿批改抄录。

　　编辑"重华报"是一件很愉快的事，姐妹俩都从中学到了很多东西。不但使她们的中文进步了，好的中文功底对学习英文也很有好处。

她们的英文都成了全班第一。自办小报，其乐无穷、得益无穷。

词汇 Words

短波	duǎn bō	short wave
信息	xìn xí	information
漫画	màn huà	cartoon
编辑	biān jí	edit
功底	gōng dǐ	skills
得益	dé yì	benefit

成语 Idiom

其乐无穷	qí lè wú qióng	fun, enjoy it endlessly

问题 Questions

[1] 雪儿和冰儿办的小报都有哪些栏目？

What columns did the tiny newspaper have?

[2] 办小报有什么好处？为什么说办中文小报对提高自己的英文水平有好处？

What are the advantages of producing a tiny newspaper?

Why do we say that editing a Chinese newspaper can benefit learning the English language?

练习 Exercises

[1] 和朋友一起，设计出一期小报来。

Design one issue of a tiny Chinese newspaper with your friends.

[2] 用"其乐无穷"造句。

Construct a sentence using the idiom "其乐无穷".

实用汉语 Practical Chinese (14)
运动 Sports

A 词汇 Words

游泳	yóu yǒng	swim
慢跑	màn pǎo	jogging
射击	shè jī	shooting
射箭	shè jiàn	archery
举重	jǔ zhòng	weightlifting
拳击	quán jī	boxing
锻炼	duàn liàn	physical exercises
竞走	jìng zǒu	heel-to-toe walking
奥林匹克	ào lín pǐ kè	Olympic
精神	jīng shén	spirit
击剑	jī jiàn	fencing
跳高	tiào gāo	high jumping
跳远	tiào yuǎn	long jumping
赛马	sài mǎ	horse racing
国际象棋	guó jì xiàng qí	chess
围棋	wéi qí	go
足球	zú qiú	soccer
排球	pái qiú	volley ball

B 对话

------ 我喜欢运动。锻炼使人健康。
Wǒ xǐ huān yuàn dòng. Duàn liàn shǐ rén jiàn kāng.
I like sports. Exercises make people healthy.

------ 你喜欢举重吗？不太喜欢，我更喜欢射箭和射击。

Nǐ xǐ huān jǔ zhòng mā? Bú tài xǐ huān, wǒ gèng xǐ huān shè jiàn hé shè jī.

Do you like weightlifting? Not really, I prefer archery and shooting.

------ 我不喜欢看拳击和击剑，看起来很危险呢。

Wǒ bù xǐ huān kàn quán jī hé jī jiàn, kàn qǐ lái hěn wēi xiǎn ne.

I do not want to watch boxing and fencing, they look so dangerous.

------ 还是竞走、游泳、赛马好看。

Hái shì jìng zǒu, yóu yǒng, sài mǎ hǎo kàn.

I think heel-to-toe walking, swimming and horse-racing are more attractive.

------ 我父亲说"活到老、走到老"，慢跑也可以锻炼人。

Wǒ fù qīn shuō "huó dào lǎo, zǒu dào lǎo", màn pǎo yě kě yǐ duàn liàn rén.

My father told us "walk always, as long as you are alive". Jogging can help people stay healthy too.

------ 坚持锻炼可以活到 100 岁。

Jiān chí duàn liàn kě yǐ huó dào yī bái suì.

Keep exercising and you may live up to 100 years old.

------ 但是我不懂为什么国际象棋或者围棋也算体育，比赛的人都坐着不动。

Dàn shì wǒ bù dǒng wèi shé mō guó jì xiàng qí huò zhě wéi qí yě suàn tǐ yù, bǐ sài de rén dōu zuò zhe bú dòng.

However, I do not understand why chess or go is a sport. The athletes just sit there not moving.

------ 但是那是比赛啊。

Dàn shì nà shì bǐ sài á.
Nevertheless, that is still a match.

------ 我明白了。让我们一起锻炼身体。
Wǒ míng bái lě. Ràng wǒ mén yī qǐ duàn liàn shēn tǐ.
I see, let us do physical exercises together.

------ 奥林匹克精神万岁！
Ào lín pǐ kè jīng shén wàn suì!
Long live the Olympic Spirit!

C 把同一意思的词用线条连起来
Match the words

足球	shè jiàn	chess
举重	guó jì xiàng qí	jogging
跳远	pái qiú	swim
围棋	màn pǎo	volleyball
击剑	yóu yǒng	weightlifting
赛马	duàn liàn	soccer
锻炼	tiào gāo	high jumping
射箭	zú qiú	archery
排球	jǔ zhòng	long jumping
慢跑	tiào yuǎn	horse racing
国际象棋	wéi qí	physical exercise
跳高	jī jiàn	go
游泳	sài mǎ	fencing

CPSIA information can be obtained
at www.ICGtesting.com
Printed in the USA
FFHW011507101219
56854152-62507FF